*In memory of my brother*

# Good Luck With That

*Don Boes*

**FUTURECYCLE PRESS**
*www.futurecycle.org*

Library of Congress Control Number: 2015932559

Copyright © 2015 Don Boes
All Rights Reserved

Published by FutureCycle Press
Lexington, Kentucky, USA

ISBN 978-1-938853-83-8

## Contents

Both Shoulders Closed ............................................................ 7
Retain This Portion for Your Records ..........................9
Sweatshirt ................................................................................. 10
Balloon ....................................................................................... 12
Critter Control ........................................................................ 13
Window Seat ............................................................................ 14
Drinking Beer in the Rain .................................................. 16
Homework ................................................................................. 17
Inheritance ............................................................................... 18
What's Left Over .................................................................... 20
Save It For a Rainy Day ...................................................... 21
Nest .............................................................................................. 22
Thank You for Calling ......................................................... 23
Monkey ....................................................................................... 24
Soft Target ................................................................................ 26
All I Want .................................................................................. 28
Shimmy ...................................................................................... 29
Groundwater ............................................................................ 30
Spillage ....................................................................................... 31
War in Spring .......................................................................... 32
Consultation ............................................................................ 34
Stars ............................................................................................. 36
Mud ............................................................................................... 37
Eavesdropping at the Henry Clay Estate ..................... 38
Disappearing Turtle .............................................................. 40
Tornado ...................................................................................... 42
Out of Bed ................................................................................. 43
Resentment .............................................................................. 44
Bedtime ...................................................................................... 45
Sweetness in Ypsilanti ......................................................... 46
Good Luck With That ........................................................... 48

Alumni Reception.................................................................. 49
Losing Streak.......................................................................50
The Old Neighborhood......................................................52
Electricity.............................................................................53
Comedy Club...................................................................... 54
History of Appliances.........................................................55
Leaving Los Angeles...........................................................56
Chairlift................................................................................58
Shovel.................................................................................. 60
Citation................................................................................ 62
Why We Have No Staples in the Office..............................64
Lessons I Learned While Unemployed...............................65
Doorknob............................................................................ 66
Fire Escape.......................................................................... 67
Nature Walk........................................................................ 68
Continental Drift.................................................................69
This Message Has Not Been Sent....................................... 70
Acknowledgments

## *Both Shoulders Closed*

During long car trips across Michigan
I point at the deer along the interstate
forced to swallow drainage
because of dislocation and drought.
The less essential the thought,
the more it bears repeating.
The mayonnaise is on the right
side of the refrigerator door.
That clock is three minutes fast.
Those troop movements
are not significant.
Throughout the homeland,
engineered crops
discombobulate honeybees,
causing them to file
the wrong flight plans.
Too many songwriters and buskers
have forsaken New Orleans.
Not all noise is music
but then neither is music.
Luckily, Audubon was a good shot.
He murdered Carolina parrots and shore larks
so he could render them in life-like poses.
The last novel I read had no narrative
but lots of punctuation and cleavage.
What else is there to consider
while you idle on the exit ramp?
If all the dictators of the world
would watch one hilarious movie,
we would have world peace.

I suggest *The Pink Panther*—
the original with Peter Sellers
and not the lame remake with Steve Martin.
A matinee might make the best sense.
At dusk, the despots could learn what matters,
feeding the pigeons and squirrels
their leftover popcorn.
From Ann Arbor to Traverse City,
I squeeze the steering wheel
in the construction zones.
I slow way down, not wanting
to incur a fine
or kill or maim anybody, especially myself.

## *Retain This Portion for Your Records*

In the courtyard of the Alamo
the shutter on my camera faltered,
so I have no documentation
of the lackluster pigeon on the table
where my wife and I attempted lunch.
Back at the ranch, utility bills and car repair data
circa 1994 feather our attic.
Appetite is visual, so we finished our meal
inside and out of range of scraggly feet
and bobbing head. Our guide
was enamored of the bullet holes
collected in the adobe, each indentation
somebody's historical misfire. The body
remembers some results better than the brain.
Once I owned three minutes of my dad
whispering a Roy Rogers tune on a cassette tape.
Now I recall not one syllable. My memory
of my memory has faded. After Santa Anna
routed the rebels, he released the women
and children, not out of decency
but so they could broadcast
details of the Mexican victory.
When the elementary school on the corner
closed after ninety-eight years,
even the crossing guard
was interviewed on the local news.

## *Sweatshirt*

Nobody clears the sidewalks.
Credit card offers stack up
in front of the slot.
When I wear my brother's sweatshirt,
the raggedy one with the trout,
I remember how he loved to fish
even though he never fished
after he discovered drinking
and lost his job at the restaurant
and stopped wearing the shirt.
Shoveling snow reminds me
of headlights teasing
a motel room curtain
and slush the color
of compromised teeth
and the feral cat I let sleep
in the backseat of my car.
My brother was younger and taller
and probably smarter than me,
although I had the better jump shot.
On the bus to school
he would polish off his homework
while I grappled with long division
at the kitchen table, chewing raw potatoes
my mother was chopping for dinner,
listening to the AM radio,
the songs loud but the commercials louder.
He never knew what he wanted,
but now that he's dead
he has everything he needs.

The sun shows up to sabotage
the afternoon gloom
and throw some light
against the cave wall.
The driveway is beginning
to be negotiable. The dripping starts.

## *Balloon*

A caboose rattles down the tracks.
Plastic bottles glitter and flash
and gripes give way
to base hits and strikeouts
and ladders against houses and picnics
assembled with warm wine. The greening

of the grid all over again. The season
is like one of those shiny unreadable
balloons snagged in the delicate branches
of a dogwood. What I am afraid of
is the ground and how eagerly

it rushes to make my acquaintance.
The fractured ground

where I run my seven-mile loop
slower every year. The ground
where malls of rubble
open for extended hours. The ground
where the lottery is news. Where
my father and mother and brother

are buried. Roller coasters and bulldozers
draw blood. Rivers flood
and too many people marry.
Most accidents happen at home,
wherever that is. I prefer winter.

The splendid lack of movement
and the promise of spring.

## Critter Control

My first kiss was like finding an animal
I did not recognize. Subsequent kisses
were raccoons frolicking in the driveway,

like me skittering from paycheck to paycheck
and pretending to stay honest. Possums
appeared on the garage roof. Muddy footprints

crisscrossed my shiny windshield. One kiss,
identified by staring through binoculars
I maintain for that particular purpose, was a three-legged cat.

## Window Seat

After leaving Massachusetts,
I will land near horse farms
in central Kentucky where the sun
turns the grass blue. Stop me
if I go too slowly. My mother
never visited an airport.
Neither did my younger brother.
Maybe my father hit the skies
a few times in the Korean War,
but he always spoke
of floating on the Pacific Ocean.
He never read *Moby Dick*
or "The Open Boat"

but he understood microcosms: base-
ment, riverbank, troop carrier.
My family will never fly
unless that's what they're doing now—
underfoot and underground—
cruising beneath the glitched radar
of memory. Who doesn't
like to disengage
from blood and fiction
to look down
on the landscape,
overwhelming and trivial?
I always request a window seat.

Even clouds flabbergast me.
Like my kids, I stare at the planes
as they disregard gravity.

Maybe that's what death is: craning
your neck, holding a ticket that's paid for,
going up and coming down,
all the while munching on tiny salted peanuts.
Maybe death is a complete list of verbs,
a thick paperback for those long layovers.
I sure hope so. There's nothing
like walking through those automatic doors—
all you need in one suitcase, everything else
in the other.

## *Drinking Beer in the Rain*

Tomorrow is soon enough to embrace
the new technology. It's not customer service
until somebody answers the phone.

Tomorrow I will put my best foot forward
and stick my neck out. The feathery
drizzle barely dimples the foam.

Tomorrow I promise to enhance
my professional skills. Committee work
and personal assessment can wait

for a brighter day. Sometimes
my pants do not match my shirt.
Slightly insane people

often appear otherwise. Too many words
mean the same thing, or nearly so.
*Funny* and *sad* are especially thorny.

To invent or discover or create
promotes friction in the office.
When it rains, I pour.

## Homework

One afternoon, scissors gashed my son's hand.
A little blood and pain and he sobbed

all the way to the emergency room
where a manager of a tobacco farm,
squinting like a drunk before lunch,

explained how he nearly lost an eye,
something about a pair of pliers and razor wire.

That night, homework added to the discomfort.
Do you know what 4 + (−3) * 2 equals?
Do you realize the capital of Monaco

is Monaco? Not all European geography
is that predictable. Flash cards don't help.

Plastic flamingos outnumber real flamingos.
You can erase and erase but the wrong answers
remain, like stitches, part of whatever's correct.

*Inheritance*

Late one grade-school night,
after I whispered a few prayers
and arranged my stuffed animals,
a thunderclap the size of the county
nearly yanked me out of my pajamas
and flung me, wrapped in a blanket,
into a preposterous skid
across the lightning-lit linoleum.

My parents and brother slept.
Morning was a rousing waste
as I tried to recapture that flash
for the sake of my family
and sway that trio of sleepers,
all of whom are now gone for good,
swaddled and buried
in boxes of my choosing.

And now, like everything else
in the inventory—like money,
like the locked and empty cedar chest—
the bed and the floor are mine.
The entire estate is mine to tabulate,
mine to boil down and divide up,
mine to plow under or rise above,
because I am the last one left,

the balance if not the surplus,
the one not sleeping, the one

with three graves to frequent
and three silver crosses
salvaged in proximate years
and in three different months,
each in its way long-suffering and extreme—
January, March, July.

## What's Left Over

Broken toe, pinched nerve in the neck,
strained ligament in one of my knees,
root canal: that's my list of highlights
so far. If I want to be comprehensive,
I can add my midnight appendectomy
and, of course, my case of gout. And as a boy
I experienced one, maybe three concussions.

So I don't attack the creepers
that cover the patio and one side of the garage
or paint the porch every four years.
So maybe that's why I am seldom loud
like my neighbors. Last night they tossed firecrackers.
They poked hissing sparklers into their own shrubs.
A few harmless bullets entertained the clouds.

What scares me is what might be heading down the pike:
bifocals and biopsies and perhaps a hearing aid
and all my chow prepared in a blender.
Others will manage the paperwork. No health plan
will cover the trepidation. And what's left over
will be no surprise: potato salad and defective fuses,
the glare and the shouts, the expense and the fallout.

## Save It For a Rainy Day

Although you may feel bothered and prickly,
it never hurts to fill out an application.

When my father died, I inherited
two or three boxes of hammers
and various jelly jars filled with nails.

My favorite shirt will be the spiffy one
chosen for me to wear at my funeral.

Luna moths are born without mouthparts.

The police officer was so soft-spoken
I requested that he repeat his suggestion
for dealing with our emergency.

I never learned to whistle.

The ugliness of a crying face.

I used to collect shoestrings.

There's a movie on TV
I've been meaning to see.

I have many memories of my childhood,
as do a lot of other people.

My daughter, when the earthquake struck,
skedaddled from the theatre without her moccasins.

Every year, near the beginning of September,
the season of autumn rolls around.

## Nest

After the bad news from the mechanic,
I stopped driving in the wrong gear.
And after I repaired my bike,
I never switched back to beer.
More information is always available,
but a word to the wise
is like that bird's nest in my garage
I can't throw away. Such a network
of industry and optimism and constructed
out of dental floss and ribbons by sparrows!
What the lawyer slides across the shiny table
is sometimes helpful, always billable.
After your wife ignores you for a week,
a promenade by the canal
is better than a backstage pass
unless a classy buffet is involved.
When you change lanes,
use your signals. In the bedroom,
make your move by candlelight
so you appear more attractive
and less accidental. To understand
my dashboard data is to understand
my manual, which I understand
is translated from Japanese to English
by an ESL student in Kentucky.
He's a major basketball junkie
and follows the ponies
and, in terms of salary,
will be trouncing me
by the end of the semester.

## *Thank You for Calling*

Unfortunately, I am not at my desk right now.
Please leave your most attractive scenario—
though so far no one has fared better
than the woman who gave me the slippers
off her feet. The hotel was by the river

and the river was preoccupied with barges.
One year later we married. You are listening
to this monologue because I am elsewhere,
sharpening pencils, running relaxed miles,
comparing apples and oranges. In other words

I am inching closer to the beginning
and closer to the end, like water that surrenders
to the drain. Even so, I still enjoy those slippers.
Nearly all information is optional. Don't hang up.
This message will repeat until the glaciers come home.

## Monkey

When a raccoon appeared on our porch
to scavenge sunflower seeds from the feeder,
I provided a second helping.
Too many hunters dot the fields,
some with pony tails, some with tattoos,
some with GPS systems, all of them
with shiny guns. So I did not like
to see the monkey on the leash at the mall.
He scampered around pylons
and traipsed up and down steps.
He drew a crowd. I say *he* because
the monkey was introduced as Alberto.
But the kids named a stray cat Lester
before we discovered she was a girl.
The name stuck. For months
Lester met me as I retrieved the newspaper.
One morning she disappeared.
Meanwhile the planet loses a language
every two weeks. After years of teaching,
I received the following excuse
for the first time: *the dog
ate my homework.* Seriously.
Why blame an animal
for your own shortcomings?
My brother accidentally struck
our family pooch with his truck.
My father carried Ace, the poor mutt,
to the garage and fired his pistol.

My brother may have been drunk. In his
collared shirt and tailored pants,
Alberto wowed the audience.
He was both in costume and not.
That monkey was so talented,
I cancelled my prescription meds.
That monkey never nibbled
the hand that nourished him.

## Soft Target

One professor, sitting cross-legged,
continues his composition class
under the skimpy tree by the stadium
while his students reckon
the number of dogs and detectives
required to respond
to a bomb threat.
The semester is weeks old
but already the football team
has lost four games, two by shutouts.

Imagine jabbering
about paragraph development
in the exasperating sun. Better yet,
imagine listening to such jabber
while volunteers with megaphones
tell stragglers to pick up the pace
or run the risk of being buried
beneath tons of rubble.
Don't all lectures make a little noise
and then go missing in the parking lot?
Only rookies think October
is too early to flunk out.

There's no explosive device,
just a chagrined sophomore
who has a few issues
with his geography syllabus
and has assembled a scale model

of the administration building
out of paperclips. He lingers on the line
in case one of his score of enemies
wants to trace the call
or say hello.

## *All I Want*

is to follow the cobblestones
down to the canal. In the rain
I am happy to be by myself

except for seagulls and graffiti.
I am not confused as to my whereabouts.
I am not lost like the last time

I searched for your house
in Osprey Cove subdivision.
After driving through the mighty gates

I turned left on Pink Pigeon Way
and then made a common mistake.
I turned left on Quail Run Road

although I should have turned right
on Eagle Creek Drive. To my credit,
I came nowhere near Pelican Valley Lane.

Now, walking on these shiny cobblestones,
I cannot count the mistakes I am making,
they are so few and so far between.

## *Shimmy*

Even when the sky is frosty,
I turn on the fan just to see the blades
go faster and faster. I have high hopes.

At top speed, the fan does a little shimmy
and I think the plastic body
will not contain the twisting.

My injured toe throbs
but I like the color, a clownish purple
that makes me want to poke it with my finger.

I hope my name is in the system.
I hope the motor I hear

is my heart. My colleagues
ask if my toe is broken. I hope
I don't burn the cookies. Sometimes

I say yes. Sometimes I say no.
My hopes are always in attendance,
spinning so rapidly you can feel the breeze.

## Groundwater

The stamp on the back of my hand
says I paid my admission
to this predicament. Why else
would I strain to read the subtitles?
My travels are epic: the cathedral,
the farmer's market, the hospital
parking garage where I get lost
trying to get well, the hardware store
where I buy curtain rods that don't fit.
Nothing confuses me like lucid directions
delivered patiently by a local.
When we were babies, we were mostly bald
and wore short pants everywhere.
Then we acquired locks and tresses
and happy hour included free appetizers.
I learned to save receipts,
and even my curveball found the strike zone.
Then our corporate sponsors dropped us
and the new paint was too thick,
the door sticking in the lower left-hand corner.
Groundwater softened the basement floor to mush.
The cat left a mangled mouse on the welcome mat
and the final consisted of material
not found on the syllabus. One red carnation
was all the furniture I could afford.
That time in the rain I should have kissed her,
but that was the wrong mistake to make.
Back in the boondocks, I fashioned a landscape
from my woe. My lips were cracked.
Her ribbons were damp, my ditches flooded.

## *Spillage*

After weeks of winter,
I venture outside with a carafe of wine
and stumble on the buckling pavement
of April. Another season of spillage.
In the school playground,
a smashed piggy bank twinkles
like late snow on the asphalt,
all the moolah gone. Who would fling
a ceramic swine, the creepy kind
with lidless eyes and red lips,
against an academy of learning and snacks?
After forty-two semesters of taking notes,
I can score in the upper percentiles
but I can't identify the plants in my backyard.
My father's perennials were thriving
when the ambulance collected him
for the last time. At the hospital
all he could do was squeeze my hand.
All I could manage was to allow
his tomatoes to ripen and fall.

## War in Spring

Instead of staring
at the bloodshed on TV,
I should concentrate
on my own yard work—
gather some branches
knocked down
by last week's storm,
straighten the brick border
around the curbside hawthorn,
and deal with the dandelions.
After the hourly bombing updates,
I'll sweep the sidewalk
and clip the ivy
to within an inch of the ground.
Although I like to see
a dictator toppled
as much as the next guy,

my fence is leaning
and my gutters
are choked with leaves.
In my spare time,
I like to avoid conflict.
When a soldier dies,
the network flashes
a yearbook photo
of the fallen one.
When the weather
turns civil,

a woodpecker
returns to the yellowwood
outside my window.
The fewer chores
I do today, the fewer
I'll do tomorrow.

## Consultation

Although my father-in-law
has been diagnosed with metastasized
prostate cancer, his wife maintains
he's just not getting any younger
and what do doctors know
anyway. The meteorologist
on the lowest-rated network
forecasts the next shower
will hit the only lake in the county
square in the eye. That's why
we subscribe to 117 channels.
Married sixty years, my in-laws
operate in an alternate universe,
one where she doesn't allow him
to finish his oatmeal
or attend Mass in his sneakers,
one where our son steals her bananas.
In high school Brother Borgia,
a math teacher who threw erasers
hard enough to leave a welt,
enlightened us with the saga
of an elderly couple
and how one of them—
I can't remember which one—
died. The remaining spouse
lingered for a week,
not long enough for the milk to turn.
*That's love,* Brother Borgia said
and cried at his desk.

He possessed an accurate aim,
and some of the marks are still there.
My father-in-law's consultation
is Friday. His wife won't go,
embarrassed to be seen in public
with her walker. He will decline
all treatment. Besides, there's a storm
on the way—anybody with a window
can see that—hospice has been notified,
and a banana thief remains loose in the world.

## *Stars*

A few weeks after Christmas,
as if we remember Christmas,
a pretty snow falls. Payments
fly through the mail and pain
is managed like the slumbering drifts.
Unopened presents remain surprises.
When I make my omelet,
I add paprika and mushrooms.
The morning my father-in-law died,
he could not tell the black pieces
from the white. Who my son was.
To the family, to the sleeping cat,
he spoke only German,
his original language on this original earth.
He mistook the caregiver for his late wife
of sixty-two years. Oxygen
arrived from a machine in the corner.
Lawrence Welk was all the rage.
No more supervising the stars
through his homemade telescope.
No more sailing in the boat
he built in the backyard.
His Morse code pitter-pattered out to sea.
Every day I do something to make me happy.
No more stars. Except for the blinky ones
in the sky, no more stars.

## *Mud*

Down under my house the river is.
The water is claiming the basement
and climbing the hill to the pharmacy,
swamping the playground, filling elevator shafts
in my office complex, floor by floor by floor
soaking the hospital where I called on my father
and then my mother and eventually my brother.
Even our mansions and mainframes are in jeopardy.
Three summers ago, canoes were the fashion
and our street the runway; the envisioned floodwall
remains a line item submerged in the town budget.

After the overflow, a burgeoning of yard sales:
clammy magazines, treasured revolvers,
radios, bicentennial paraphernalia.
Every object is earmarked by mud
like anger sometimes shadows sadness.
You can scrape it off if you decide to buy.

## *Eavesdropping at the Henry Clay Estate*

Even those blue parachute-shaped clouds
on that Tuesday before Thanksgiving
suggested some kind of risk, a proposal.
Their voices, hushed but enthusiastic,
sounded like golf commentators on TV.
*I had no idea, I had no idea,*
the woman said. She repeated the phrase
while her sweetie—and I'm not making this up—
knelt before her to better display the ring,
a token so replete with symbolic baggage
he could barely slip it on her finger.
But slip it on he did. All this I witnessed.
Where we were—a nineteenth-century
estate restored by the local
garden club—was brilliant. A sundial
here, a cherub there, lots of gravel
and ivy, nothing fancy. Now I wish
I knew how my parents decided to marry.

Now I wish I had asked. As the two pilgrims
walked arm-in-arm out the rusty gates,
plans already formed on their lips.
Imagine that. Sometimes a light shines.
Sometimes a moment is so private
everybody understands. Suddenly I panicked.
Will they invite me to the wedding?
And since I am a stranger to both bride and groom,
whatever present will be appropriate?

Such a gift is never easy to choose.
Maybe they will appreciate a calendar
since the new year is so near. She said yes.
Did I mention she said yes?
Maybe a wildlife calendar. Maybe
a calendar of historic locales.
She said yes numerous times. *Yes. Yes.
Yes.* After a while I stopped counting.
*Yes. Yes.* I stopped. *Yes.*

## *Disappearing Turtle*

Not much remains of the turtle
I found last week on Queensway Drive
except a few shards of the shell,
just enough for some sharp-eyed kid
to take to school for extra credit.
My strategy was to capture the animal
to show my two turtle-crazy children
and then release it in the reservoir.
Only when I slowly picked it up
did I realize the creature had no head.
Now, more than the head is not there.
Sometimes the inside goes away before the outside.
Eighteen months in our house, and yesterday
I noticed a crack in the living room wall
between a window and the fireplace.
Another woe to discuss with a professional

or plaster over by myself. The house
is fifty-five years old, so I don't know
if it is falling apart or falling apart
gracefully. And while I'm on the subject,
my brother died from the inside out,
all of him condemned by thirty-three.
He was weary by then, and quite experienced,
as he liked to tell me during his alcoholic
lectures. Today I called my two-year-old son,
Simon, by the name of Possum Paws. That's
what my father called me
because of my little hands.

Simon never met my father or brother.
He's never gone face-to-face with a turtle,
even a headless one. He has little hands like me
and, like me, he won't let go.

## Tornado

That freak tornado skipped my county,
but east and south the power is out.
My IQ drops as my kids grow up—
Mark Twain said something like that.
Back in the day, I provided exact quotes
and assembled appropriate pants-shirt combos
but, now, not so much. Lost books
I no longer replace. Missed belt loops
do not indicate something. I used to floss.
At banquets I leave before dessert
and at mass I sneak out after communion.
My hotel is cheap but my pillow
is fluffy. Or my bagel is steep
and her confetti is huffy.
A storm-blown baby
found alive in a field
died the next day. Damage
appears on the uninsured faces
of her parents. I was wrong,
really way off base, about the sex
of that stray cat. My wife
I love like a balanced checkbook.
After more or less dodging debris,
who wants to tackle homework?
Everybody is somebody I used to know.

## Out of Bed

What gets me out of bed
is the pleasure of eating cornflakes
with the spoon I discovered
in the casino parking lot.
It was spring and the asphalt
bloomed with yellow lines
and stenciled numerals.
Whatever is true must be exaggerated
to be believed. Too many people
spend weeks staring at the wrong data,
neglecting their diets,
their appearances suffering.
I would rather plummet from the apex
of the loftiest nomenclature
than create a new password
or decorate one more cubicle
in a personal style.
I would rather not
earn another degree.
On the way down
I will count my chickens
and complete my top-secret journal.
When I hit the loamy earth,
my first and last pillow in this life,
my eyes will be open.

*Resentment*

runs high as an ambulance
disrupts traffic. The guy in the next lane
clobbers his steering wheel with his fist
because the light is green
and his SUV is going nowhere.

Surrounded by leather and digital sound,
he flinches and gripes.

I have been the steering wheel. I have been the fist.

Most people on the planet do not own a car.

## Bedtime

Those pennies that congregate in jelly jars,
that stack of quarters marked for machine slots,

the check forever cruising through the mail,
even that two-dollar bill tucked inside a birthday card—

all of it lies down as we do,
faces and edges softening,

not knowing what it looks like,
smart money relaxing with the foolish,

paper napping with coin, every moment a luxury.

## Sweetness in Ypsilanti

The trainee at the front desk
gives me a disagreeable rate. Thanks
to a high school soccer team
and a shrill ice machine, dissonance
is standard in every room.
Who knew Ypsilanti
could be so raucous?
The hullabaloo in my own head
won't go away—climbing the stairs
I think of ladders,
especially my father's
wooden stepladder

I gave away
in my third or fourth life
since he died. Now
when I need to change the bulb
in the walk-in closet
or clear the neighbor's
tree branches off my garage roof,
I'm ladderless and small.
Now aluminum and fiberglass
is the stuff of ladders. My father
bedecked his device
in leftover blue

and carved his name
on the top step. At least
the way up is still vertical,
as is the way down.

With alacrity I fire up
the complimentary java.
I stroke the piece of soap
in its dish and admire
the piece of art
hung like a fast-food menu
over my bed. There's
sweetness in every rung.

## Good Luck With That

What bothers me is my underground masterpiece
and how I can't seem to finish it.
Right now I fear my masterpiece
is not appropriately languid
or rotationally sound, at least not for my taste.
In the hospital gift shop, the ceramic animals,
even though they traveled all the way from China,
fail to lift my spirits. Although
we were promised jetpacks,
we were gifted with my masterpiece.
When I venture forth for dinner,
my supporters never implore me
to sign their napkins. If only
I could practice such discipline
as I ponder my masterpiece.
In the back of the book, I look for the answers.
And when I ran over the snake in the crosswalk,
I understood that my audience
would be disappointed in my judgment.
Some questions do not require question marks.
My picnic in the industrial park
failed for a number of reasons.
Tomorrow I will maximize several new ideas.
Already I worry about airport security
and if my masterpiece will arouse suspicion.

## *Alumni Reception*

Outside the November sun
and, inside, appetizers and aquaponics,
and I'm wearing black and gold
to broadcast my school spirit,
and is that Larry talking to the development officer
or Larry's younger brother
or maybe David's odd roommate
from sophomore year? Higher
education is a wonderful thing
but, in the event of an earthquake,
follow the nearest elephant.
An early-season contest
between in-state rivals,
the game promises to be close,
our slick guard play
a counter to their senior forwards,
their average ACT scores
matched against our endowment.
The last time I visited the campus
I had to use a map. Each of us
knows a lot about something,
but my paperbacks from British Lit
are falling to pieces. The quarterly newsletter
reports less and less
of our class gossip. Four of my professors
are still alive. I snag
a keychain and two bumper stickers.
In the trampled snow,
we don't know
how to say goodbye.

## *Losing Streak*

This morning my neighbor
chainsawed his sorry apple tree
all the way to the ground.
He's an assistant basketball coach,
newly fired by the university,
his tiny headshot

stuck at the bottom
of the newspaper column
documenting the latest loss.

Now he can admire
the lopsided water tower
on the next block, and so can I.
Like Yogi Berra declared,
it's amazing what you can observe
just by watching. I was lucky,
after weeks of rummaging,
to locate Duchamp's nude
descending the staircase.

Her dainty cubist mouth
still escapes me. By no means
does she resemble Scarlett Johansson,

so my disappointment is great.
Mushy apples plastered his driveway
regardless of the season.
No replacement has been named

and the losing streak continues.
A national search is likely.
All my information
comes from junk mail

and open sky
and sawdust.

## The Old Neighborhood

Remember the road trip
from Louisville to Cleveland
to visit Michelle (we called
her Mickey) and to see
the Indians play the Royals
in the Mistake by the Lake?
Long ago reduced to rubble,
that stadium. So what else is new?
Those bleacher seats are dust
and Mickey was dead of a flustered heart
weeks after we headed south.
She adored *A Confederacy of Dunces*.

The new owner of my childhood home
has cut down the tree in the front yard,
the tree in the front yard of the house
I will always never live in again.
Now that address is treeless,
although my memory
still provides song and shade
and summer afternoons
with my little brother
surrounded by a chain-link fence.
Whether guilty or not so guilty,
we all want more polish
applied to our permanent record.
After my brother died,
I found a pistol under his sofa.
Mickey, by the way, bicycled
across the kingdom of Spain.
She sat next to me in right field.

## *Electricity*

January and all my resolutions
are replaced by daydreams of travel—
the last few weeks uniquely stressed
by favored teams losing their nerve,
my cousin, intoxicated,
blindsiding my aunt's Christmas tree,
and me, like my father,
stalking the kids from floor to floor,
turning off lamps and lecturing,
lecturing about the waste of energy,
the burning of something called money.

All the cable channels say go somewhere
novel, somewhere invigorating.
Nova Scotia, I think, is like that.
Alaska. Or we could stay home.
*I don't know the cost of electricity,*
*but if nobody is in the room*
*I want all the lights off.* That's
what my dad used to say. That's
the template for my future.
Just a few ornaments were destroyed,
but they were old and not replaceable.

## Comedy Club

Like chickens, punch lines come and go.
Local commercials are funnier. To save his life,
the King of Gadgets hyperventilates,
his pitch loaded with plain talk.
No silly clothes are necessary.
We get the point. We pay a cover charge
to grin at jokes told deep in flickering lounges.

We like to hear our laughter
before it's obsolete, before we realize
all comedy claims a victim
and before we turn helpless,
our timing wrecked or gone.
Whatever replaces laughter will be no bargain.
Whatever replaces laughter will be deafening

and offer no relief because it will never stop.
After the second encore,
the comedian steps away
from the microphone
and applause trickles
toward the now-trivial stage.
We leave small but generous tips.

## *History of Appliances*

When she left me, I behaved badly.
I disabled the refrigerator
and wore flip-flops to social functions.
Mostly I failed to pay attention.
Whatever's arranged on the dinner plate
is not guaranteed to be nourishing
or even food. When my stove melted,
the fire department responded
by yanking the cooling metal
out of the kitchen wall
and dropping it on the patio.
They checked for hot spots.
Some gentleman with a truck
salvaged it the next day.
I have never attempted a marathon
or received a heart transplant.
Garbage disposals are smarter
and dishwashers know your name.
I climbed the Great Wall
and display the certificate.
I saw a cat on a leash. 106.
That's how many times "and so it goes"
appears in *Slaughterhouse-Five*.
I like to read, but I don't bother to understand.
After surviving the fire-bombing of Dresden in 1945,
Vonnegut tripped over his adopted daughter's Lhasa apso,
hit his head, and never regained consciousness.
His X-rays were ugly, and he died at eighty-four.
My new stove includes sixty pages of instructions.
In a few weeks, I hope to boil water.

## Leaving Los Angeles

Now the franchise plays in St. Louis,
but I still wear the Los Angeles T-shirt
I gave my brother for his birthday,
years before his teeth and skin turned yellow
and he ordered fast food for a basement
full of his buddies who were not really there.
That same yellow leaked from the only highway fatality
I ever saw, a pharmacist from Nicholasville, a man
who stumbled into the path of a jalopy. Liquid
still trickled so I looked away, first at a bulldozer,
then a pile driver, then a cement mixer—anything mechanical
instead of mushy. I'm a casual fan. Every season
it's harder to know what team represents which city.
Baltimore escaped to Indianapolis to frolic in a dome.
Cleveland fled the snowy lakeside for Baltimore
and, for whatever reason, Houston relocated to Nashville.

My brother left town once in his adult life
to visit St. Louis for a fishing show.
In a rush of leisure, he stopped along the interstate
and dropped a line into what must have been drainage
or a slumping puddle of a pond. One Christmas,
though he was nearly sober, he scared my daughter
by talking too loud and repeating himself. Every evening
it's harder to tell my daughter no runaway linebacker
will flatten her, that no keystroke-quick monster
plans to jump out of nowhere or somewhere.

Every evening before her head hits the pillow,
it's nearly impossible to tell her anything. She's seven.
At least she wasn't with me to see the sheet-shaped body.

My brother died before the Rams moved to St. Louis
and before most of the rest of his life. In his last days
he cheered for no team, his internal functions shut down,
tubes sluicing to and from whatever organs were left,
even the rubbernecker in me turning away.

## *Chairlift*

If you want to consider the outcroppings
at a constant speed,
then by all means lower the bar
and ride the chairlift
to the top of the ridge
and back down to the parking lot.
Before you disembark, you still have to decide
who to leave what. Who is who and what is what
are just two of the questions.
Obtaining a cemetery plot
is a sound investment
if you stop breathing next week
but if you inhabit the earth
another twenty-five years, maybe not so much.
By then your kids will be adults
with a bunch of embarrassing and useful memories,
your house will need fresh paint,
and your river will require new craft.
Resist sleeping in the afternoon,
although what the comedian said
is true if not hilarious:
hard work pays off in the future
and laziness pays off now.
Temperatures are rising
and the oceans are rising
and so long Bangkok and Shanghai and Miami.
We're buying smaller phones
and bigger televisions, and I have no clue
where to find a flashlight.

Three of my colleagues retired this spring
and others are sporting canes
and new hips, thankful
for the lesser injuries and ailments,
the stairs not too taxing. Deep pockets help.
So I keep my introductions short.
I refuse the elevator, the escalators,
the motorized sidewalk.

## *Shovel*

Predicting the future is easy.
All I need is a shovel
so I can bury a possum
discovered in the driveway.
Just like flipping a calendar
from one month of gadgets
to the next. July features
a combination clock and toaster
and August offers a taser
matched with an MP3 player.
Since my speedometer is busted
I'm rolling toward the horizon
at zero miles per hour—
solid news if you ask me.
All thunder and no rain.
Orville Wright lived to see
airlines provide in-flight movies.
Junked laptops and monitors
are stacked to the rafters
of the warehouse. No wonder
my searches produce so few hits!
All blunder and no pain.
In general, U-turns are prohibited.
The tail of the possum
sticks out of the ground
like a damaged antenna.
A little technology goes a long way.
A real mechanic listens
to the alternator and the muffler.

All of us grin and chatter
and think we make sense.
Years ago, I spent evenings
like this on my front porch
following the Reds on the radio,
charmed by crickets and swallows.
A thin-lipped snout
is all that's left to cover.
A happy ending depends
on where you stop the story.
A headstone can commemorate
a life or mark a grave.
On top I leave a heavy rock.

*Citation*

According to the city government,
our boxwoods obstruct the view
of our street address
and so we are in violation
of the Code of Ordinance,
Chapter 17, Article 1,
Section 2-4. On a daily basis
our obscured signage
presents a hardship
to pizza delivery people
and emergency personnel.
I would do the clipping myself
but I lack the proper tools
and expertise. That's everybody's story.
Even so, the Apollo 13 astronauts,
after a zany oxygen tank explosion
200,000 miles from earth,
safely splashed down
in the Pacific near Samoa.
One time I drove toward Kentucky
but hit some other state,
probably Ohio. Who wants
a cold sausage and pineapple
with extra cheese
is a rhetorical question.
What feels like hunger
is often thirst. Who wants
to be responsible
for a pair of lost paramedics?

We have three weeks
to comply with the citation
before the penalties,
on an incremental basis, kick in.

## Why We Have No Staples in the Office

According to Lisa's report
the tsunami also caused
a shortage of components
which is why
we have no staples in the office.

## *Lessons I Learned While Unemployed*

Crowd the coffee table with coffee.
Pay a visit to every booth in the bar.

According to lots of presidents and pro athletes
hardships are in fact opportunities.

Scan the local swimming pool
for bumblebees in distress
and old high school friends
who might also bother the surface,
buzzing, with something like panic.
A simple net at the end of a long handle
often does the trick.

Sometimes I am not bored enough.
The phone lines are open.

All my best ideas
happen to be your ideas.
All I require are your last four digits.
Will you stay for dinner?
I have microscopic fish to fry.

## Doorknob

The instructions for the new doorknob
say to replace the old doorknob
with the new doorknob.
The second-best way to acknowledge
the burn at the back of your throat
is to open a book and memorize
the white space where the words stop.
Multiple exposures will increase your understanding.
The best way is more whiskey. No skill
is required to toss a twitching fish
back into the water, no matter
how brackish the water, no matter
the glop on your fingers. No matter
if you miss the last trolley
and walk home through one of those neighborhoods
where pay phones ring on every other corner
and where only a few stray animals appear healthy.
No skill in answering a phone or saving a fish
or just showing up. I appreciate everything,
especially hygiene products, I get in the mail for free.
That little girl in the waiting room
claimed she was hissing like a jaguar
but she sounded like an espresso machine.
Frustration grows best under fluorescent light.
My father always carried two screwdrivers—
one a Phillips and one a flathead—
because you never know. Only a knucklehead
is perplexed when a doorknob pops off in his hand.

## *Fire Escape*

Blocks away from the bar I notice her:
three stories tall with fetching eyes
and long straight hair
the color of a fire escape,
she holds in the palm of her hand
a bubble of some sort
with a creature of some sort
inside the bubble.
The establishment is closed
but the woman's eyes are open,
the solid black pupils
eclipsing the brick red
left over from early last century
when all you could order was craft beer.
The creature might be next year's coveted toy.
Although the door is locked,
the neon sign blinks and blinks
and I can only imagine what's on tap.
The creature might be a marsupial.
Her eyes might be those
of my second or third girlfriend,
but not the fourth. But the health report
posted on the window is splendid,
97 out of 100, a perfect score
foiled by a few mouse droppings
and unwrapped plastic utensils and a gasket
the new guy forgot to fix.
Tomorrow may the edifice
be open so that my thirst may be slaked.
Public art really makes you think.

## Nature Walk

At the trailhead, the ranger
allowed me, under his supervision,
to stroke the feathers of a raptor.
Until then I never understood
why the skink abandons its tail
or how dollar signs are born
or why my daughter was moving to Japan.
I was just one more sweaty hiker
meandering around in borrowed boots
while nuthatches and chickadees
napped out of sight. The fiddle music
from Hoedown Island was my least favorite part.
People like me struggled with paddleboats
and disturbed the turtles. The threat of fire
was moderate to high, the drought in full swing
and the plane departing for Chicago
and then San Francisco and on to Yokohama.
Now my breakfast will be her late-night snack.
I wish us both the best of luck.
My favorite part of the program
was when the cave went black,
although what I hoped was humility
in the face of the fossil record
turned out to be back spasms.
Another sunrise sailed into Tokyo Bay.

## *Continental Drift*

The runners left on base have long since retired.
One fewer uncle appears at the Christmas bash,
and my cat no longer vaults
from kitchen counter to refrigerator.
What used to be a bakery is now a craft brewery
outfitted with lots of glass and aluminum.
After the first seven miles, my hamstring throbs.
Experts shampoo the carpets
and amateurs water the plants.
One time I drove to Kalamazoo in a snowstorm.
The space between me and everything else
is guesswork. Today I labor
way below sea level
in a delta prone to flooding
while the Himalayas are still creeping skyward.
Yesterday I was farther away from the liquor store.
The older I get, the faster I was.
The little notebook I keep is mostly empty of ideas,
although I like the idea of keeping a little notebook.
The crust of the earth is not stable. Every year Europe
and North America move one inch farther apart,
although uncanny jazz still reaches us from Finland.
The youngest kid always gets to distribute the presents,
mostly sweaters and calendars and pajamas.
Once it was my job and I took it seriously.
My last winter in Indiana was not only cold.

## This Message Has Not Been Sent

How much banjo music is appropriate?
Will any number of banjo tunes
save me from death? How many
episodes of *Seinfeld* should I acquire?
Will the complete collection rescue me
from the grave? What about plastic Godzillas?
Driving somewhere to get to the middle
of nowhere is for the most part
unnecessary. When the shooter,
sadly off his meds, opens fire
in the lobby of the post office,
the patrons are startled
but not surprised. Every crash
is a rough correction of the graph.
Tomorrow the guy will be a celebrity,
but for now your task
is to hide behind the stamp machine.
Allow the first responders
to step over the casualties
and neutralize the suspect.
Pursue the horizon, not like railroad tracks
but like an outsider artist
or like the cloud of wasps
that chased me from the woodpile
behind my garage. I fell down—
which turned out to be an excellent strategy.
Only nineteen bites did I tally.

And the gross swelling of my features
guaranteed much sympathy. But no path
is as direct as the one we are traveling,
the way not even Lazarus
could completely escape, the trail
beginning from now.

## Acknowledgments

*ABZ:* "Drinking Beer in the Rain," "Resentment"
*Burnside Review:* "Doorknob"
*Cider Press Review:* "Window Seat"
*Cincinnati Review:* "Groundwater"
*Crazy Horse:* "Mud," "Inheritance"
*Hayden's Ferry Review:* "Homework"
*Kentucky Philological Review:* "Bedtime"
*Louisville Review:* "Sweetness in Ypsilanti," "Sweatshirt"
*Limestone:* "Soft Target"
*Marlboro Review:* "Leaving Los Angeles"
*New Madrid:* "War in Spring," "Losing Streak"
*Southern Indiana Review:* "Eavesdropping at the Henry Clay Estate"
*The Cape Rock:* "Balloon"
*Wisconsin Review:* "Disappearing Turtle"

I gratefully acknowledge the support of the Kentucky Arts Commission.

My thanks to Gaby Bedetti for her love and support, especially her love.

*Cover photo by Don Boes; author photo by Gaby Bedetti; cover and interior book design by Diane Kistner; Melior text and titling*

## About FutureCycle Press

FutureCycle Press is dedicated to publishing lasting English-language poetry books, chapbooks, and anthologies in both print-on-demand and Kindle editions. Founded in 2007 by long-time independent editor/publishers and partners Diane Kistner and Robert S. King, the press incorporated as a nonprofit in 2012. A number of our editors are distinguished poets and writers in their own right, and we have been actively involved in the small press movement going back to the early seventies.

The FutureCycle Poetry Book Prize and honorarium is awarded annually for the best full-length volume of poetry we publish in a calendar year. Introduced in 2013, our Good Works projects are anthologies devoted to issues of universal significance, with all proceeds donated to a related worthy cause. Our Selected Poems series highlights contemporary poets with a substantial body of work to their credit; with this series we strive to resurrect work that has had limited distribution and is now out of print.

We are dedicated to giving all of the authors we publish the care their work deserves, making our catalog of titles the most diverse and distinguished it can be, and paying forward any earnings to fund more great books.

We've learned a few things about independent publishing over the years. We have also evolved a unique, resilient publishing model that allows us to focus mainly on vetting and preserving for posterity the most books of exceptional quality without becoming overwhelmed with bookkeeping and mailing, fundraising activities, or taxing editorial and production "bubbles." To find out more about what we are doing, come see us at www.futurecycle.org.

# The FutureCycle Poetry Book Prize

All full-length volumes of poetry published by FutureCycle Press in a given calendar year are considered for the annual FutureCycle Poetry Book Prize. This allows us to consider each submission on its own merits, outside of the context of a contest. Too, the judges see the finished book, which will have benefitted from the beautiful book design and strong editorial gloss we are famous for.

The book ranked the best in judging is announced as the prize-winner in the subsequent year. There is no fixed monetary award; instead, the winning poet receives an honorarium of 20% of the total net royalties from all poetry books and chapbooks the press sold online in the year the winning book was published. The winner is also accorded the honor of being on the panel of judges for the next year's competition; all judges receive copies of all contending books to keep for their personal library.

www.ingramcontent.com/pod-product-compliance
Lightning Source LLC
LaVergne TN
LVHW020938090426
835512LV00020B/3416